close
again

close again

ELLA FRANCES SANDERS

Andrews McMeel
PUBLISHING®

This is a small collection
of longing, and of
hope. It wasn't a
plan, but I had
a sort of pain in
my chest, and
these drawings have
helped.

(I miss you.)

STANDING IN MUSEUMS
AND GALLERIES

Several years ago I traveled to Göteborg alone because it was my birthday. On a Sunday I went to the main art museum in the city and it was so empty I felt like the only person there.

I associate bus reading
of all kinds most
strongly with Seattle.

READING THE SAME
BOOK AS SOMEONE
ON THE BUS

HANDING PEOPLE
THINGS THEY'VE DROPPED

There is an impossible
intimacy to be found
when two people
kneel to pick up
dropped things.

Missed like
the sun is missed
in northern
    hemisphere winters.

BEING IN LIBRARIES
AND BOOKSTORES

CONSOLING
A STRANGER

This does not
happen enough because
people are not sure
what to say.

It is the small things
that accumulate to
make up a life — multi-
generational toothbrushing,
the first time we see
   a sibling's newborn
baby, walking the
streets of everyday
love.

SHARED ROUTINES
OF THE BEAUTIFULLY
MUNDANE VARIETY

MAKING EYE CONTACT
WITH SOMEBODY IN
A PASSING CAR

It is difficult
not to have the
sense that
you _know_ a
stranger in this
moment.

In a city where I
lived for a time there
was a tiny old cinema
in an old building,
with tiny stairs up to
the top floor.

It was always good
to go alone.

CINEMAS IN THE DARK
(AND THEATERS)

GIVING DIRECTIONS

I am not good at
this because I do not
remember most street
names. Instead I say,
"Turn left by the
tree that smells
like October."

I am surprised
that   I miss this.
But I do.

BEING PRESSED TOGETHER
ON PUBLIC TRANSPORTATION

RUNNING INTO PEOPLE
YOU KNOW IN FAR
AWAY PLACES

Ah, the smallness of it all, the ways in which we travel away from everything only to run into our neighbor in the Australian Outback.

The small fizz
of another human's
palm.

HANDSHAKES
(USUALLY AWKWARD)

STANDING IN LINE
AT THE POST OFFICE

I have been to
many post offices.
I like them all—
they usually sing
of the past.

A closeness
enhanced by the
dampness of clothing
and the delays
to destinations.

SHELTERING IN DOORWAYS
IN THE RAIN

DISCOVERING
UNEXPECTED AND
UNUSUAL PLACES

Best when also
slightly lost
with you.

The time spent in
grocery stores can be
very charming.

Perhaps it is the orderliness
of the shelves, the dances
to avoid other people near
the yogurt, the way we
always lose each other
in the aisles.

WHISPERED CONVERSATIONS
AT THE GROCERY STORE

LOOKING OUT OF
SHARED TRAIN WINDOWS

There are no trains
where I live now;
they stopped running
about 60 years ago.
Train windows provide
a singular way
to think about time
and place, and
it always felt like
my eyes were well-
exercised.

Oh! to find
oneself reaching
for the same
cabbage!

REACHING FOR
THE SAME THING
AS SOMEONE ELSE
AND BRUSHING
THEIR HAND

OFFERING TO SHARE
YOUR LUNCH

We feel the
absence of glimpses.

Humanity takes
chances here —
good chances,
bad chances.

WAITING AT BUS STOPS

HUGS-AS-HELLOS

Well, yes.

I also like to compliment people's hats.

COMPLIMENTING SOMEONE'S
SHOES WHILE WAITING AT
AN APPOINTMENT

GREETING BEAUTIFUL DOGS

Is there anything
that starts more
conversations
than a dog?

At one time it
was a job of mine
to lock up a
laundromat at night.
It was one of the
more perfect times
in my life.

WAITING AT

LAUNDROMATS

FALLING IN LOVE
WITH STRANGERS
AT COFFEE SHOPS

(Falling in love
with everything
generally .)

At the moment a
lot of days don't
make   sense. I run
out of postage stamps,
or I run out of pencil
erasers, or I find myself
running out of feelings.
This will pass, yes, but I
suspect this time will be felt,
like a leftover bruise,
for longer than we
might   imagine.

That is OK,
though – the planet
is waiting to hold
you (close) in its arms.

ellafrancessanders . com
@ ellafsanders

Andrews McMeel Publishing
a division of Andrews McMeel Universal
1130 Walnut Street, Kansas City, Missouri 64106

www.andrewsmcmeel.com

21 22 23 24 25 SDB 10 9 8 7 6 5 4 3 2 1

ISBN: 978-1-5248-7130-7

Library of Congress Control Number: 2021938772

Editor: Patty Rice
Art Director: Tiffany Meairs
Production Editor: Meg Daniels
Production Manager: Tamara Haus

ATTENTION: SCHOOLS AND BUSINESSES
Andrews McMeel books are available at quantity discounts with bulk purchase
for educational, business, or sales promotional use. For information, please
e-mail the Andrews McMeel Publishing Special Sales Department:
specialsales@amuniversal.com.